THE STORY OF THE EARTH
LAKE

LIONEL BENDER

FRANKLIN WATTS
New York · London · Toronto · Sydney

© 1989 Franklin Watts

First published in the USA by
Franklin Watts Inc.
387 Park Avenue South
New York. N.Y. 10016

US ISBN: 0 531 10708 6
Library of Congress Catalog Card
No: 87 51613

Printed in Belgium

Consultant Dougal Dixon

Designed by Ben White

Picture research by Jan Croot

Prepared by Lionheart Books
10 Chelmsford Square
London NW10 3AR

Illustrations:
Peter Bull Art

Photographs
T. Bridges/Dr Waltham 12
GeoScience Features *cover*, 7, 9, 10 , 11, 14, 15,
18, 24, 29
Heather Angel 19
J. Middleton/Dr Waltham 21
Robert Harding 8
Survival Anglia1, 17, 27
Swiss Tourist Office 22
ZEFA 25, 26, 28

THE STORY OF THE EARTH

LAKE

LIONEL BENDER

CONTENTS

This book tells the story of a typical lake. A lake is a stretch of water surrounded on all sides by land. The lake starts as a hollow in the ground. The hollow may have been formed by a glacier, by the downward movement of surface rocks, or by a landslide blocking off the lower end, or mouth, of a valley.

▽ The illustration shows a landscape with lakes at different stages of development. In the mountains there are hollows being ground out by glaciers. Downhill a lake fills with water from rivers. On the lowland is a marshy area that was once a lake. Next to this is farmland with soil formed from lake mud.

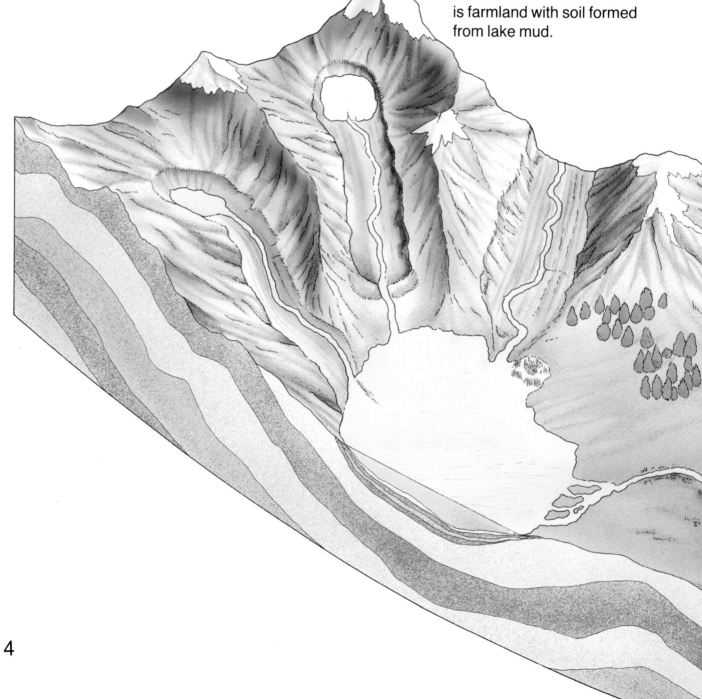

The water that fills a lake may be rain water, or it may come from a river or from the melting ice of a glacier. With time, the level of the water in the lake falls and the lake fills with mud and dead plants. It eventually becomes marshland and then dry land, with a soil so rich and fertile that it can be used for farming.

▽ We have divided the story of our lake into ten stages. In the following pages of the book we look at each stage in turn. There are photographs of lakes in different parts of the world. Diagrams explain how a lake forms and changes with time. We also look at the wildlife of lakes and how lakes affect people.

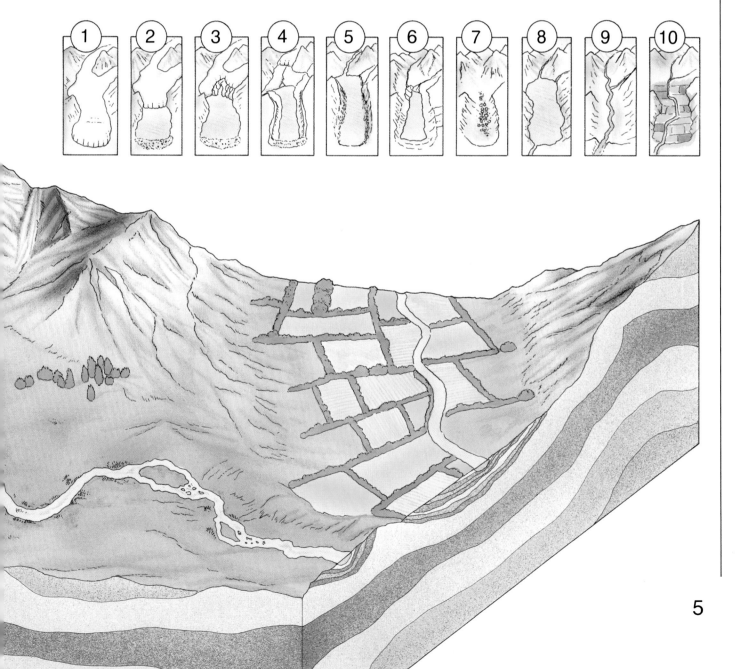

1 2 3 4 5 6 7 8 9 10

High up in the mountains, where it is very cold, the snow that falls fills every hollow. The lower layers of snow are squeezed into ice. A river of ice, or glacier, forms in a large valley. This solid mass of ice is so heavy that it starts to move downhill. Its great weight presses downward and grinds out the valley floor, scooping out rocks and boulders. Rocks trapped within the ice scrape away at the valley sides and floor. Gradually, the valley floor is worn into a deep hollow.

▷ The force of a glacier moving downhill can be seen in this photograph of the Aletsch Glacier in Switzerland. The surface of the glacier is cracked and twisted by pressures within the ice, and it carries ribbons of rocks torn from the valley sides. Deep beneath its surface, the glacier is grinding out hollows that one day will contain lakes.

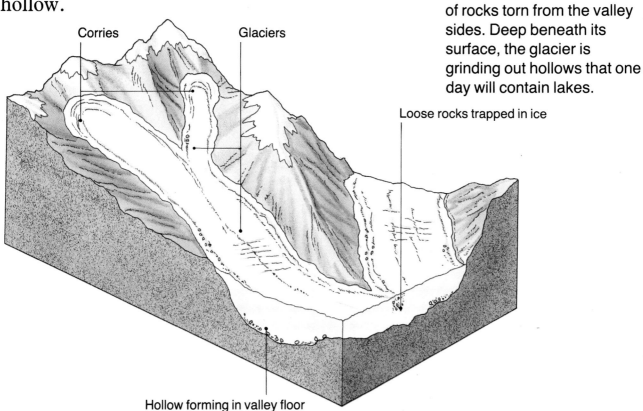

Corries

Glaciers

Loose rocks trapped in ice

Hollow forming in valley floor

△ Glaciers form in bowl-shaped rock hollows called corries or cirques. As more and more snow fills each corrie, ice forms, and this scours out the corrie bottom.

Lakes form in corries where the ice has melted. Other lakes form further down the glacier valley in hollows scraped out by the moving ice.

With warmer weather, the ice begins to melt. The ice at the tip of the glacier melts first. Water collects at the sides of the glacier and around big rocks buried in the ice. Small rocks buried in the glacier drop to the ground from the melting ice and form a barrier across the valley floor.

As the glacier melts away more and more, a large hollow in the valley floor becomes uncovered. Water from the melting ice runs downhill in small streams and begins to fill the hollow. The lake has started to form.

▷ Water pouring from the melting end of a glacier fills a mountain lake. Usually this meltwater forms river channels beneath the ice and emerges from a tunnel or cave in the tip of the glacier.

▽ As the glacier melts away, it leaves behind mounds of rocks, called moraine. These mounds can form dams that hold back the water of the lake. Sometimes a block of ice becomes trapped in the moraine. When it melts it forms a hollow in the rocky dam. This fills with water and forms a "kettle hole."

Water flowing from the melting glacier is not clean and clear. It is a milky color and looks dirty and murky. This is because it is full of grit, sand and loose soil, or silt, that the ice has scraped away from the valley floor.

These tiny pieces of rock are washed into the lake. Here they settle on the bottom, or floor, of the lake and form a layer of grit, or sediment.

▷ The rock fragments that are washed out of a melting glacier are clearly seen here at Bersaerkerbrae Glacier in Greenland. They have built up into a fan-shaped mass in front of a lake. Meltwater has cut grooves in the mass. This has created a delta – an area of gravel banks and water channels – at the base of the glacier, which is known as kame.

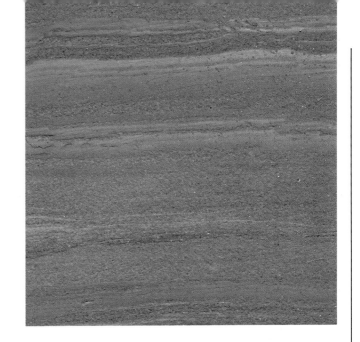

▷ In the winter, when a river is most full of water, large pieces of grit are washed into a lake. In the summer, river water carries only fine grains of sand and silt. Sediment on the lake floor builds up in the bands of coarse and fine grit known as varves. In this sediment from a lake in Essex, England, each varve is 15 cm (6 in) thick.

As the glacier continues to melt away, the lake fills with more water. The level of the water in the lake gets higher. Then, as the melting ice uncovers a side entrance to the valley, some of the water flows away.

The water level in the lake falls. Around the sides of the lake, a shelf of sand, or beach, now shows where the water used to be.

◁ The Parallel Roads of Glen Roy, in Scotland, are the beaches of an old ice-dammed lake. A lake filled the valley at the end of the Ice Age, some 370,000 years ago. As the ice melted away it uncovered different entrances to the valley and the water poured away a little at a time.

▽ A hollow in a valley is filled by water from a melting glacier (1). The overflow runs off as a river at one point. As the ice melts away it may uncover another, lower, entrance to the valley. The overflow now runs away through this, and the level of water in the lake gets lower (2). If the melting ice uncovers a third, yet lower, entrance, the water will drain away through that. Thus, the lake surface will be at a lower level still and the previous surfaces will be marked by beach lines (3).

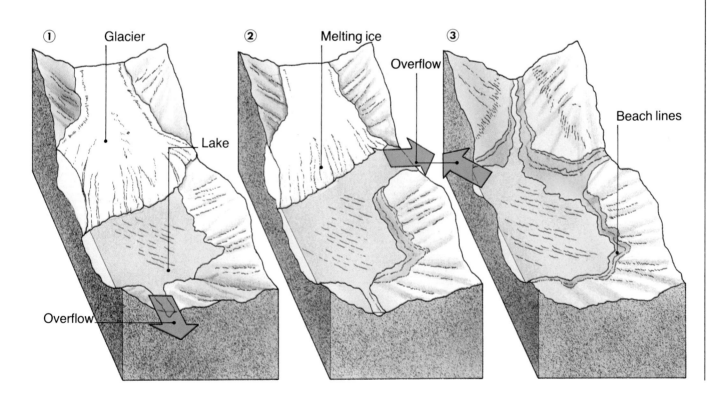

① Glacier   Lake   Overflow

② Melting ice   Overflow

③ Beach lines

Rain water and meltwater which fill the lake contain chemicals that make the sediment on the lake floor a suitable place for plants to grow.

Tiny plants, blown by the wind or carried by birds, settle in the lake and multiply. Seeds of larger plants are also carried into the water. They sprout and start growing in the sediment. Once they are established, plant-eating animals can live in the lake. These attract meat-eating animals. The lake comes alive.

▽ In the shallow water at the edges of a lake in an old glacier valley, reeds and rushes grow in large clumps. In slightly deeper water, plants such as water lilies grow. These root in the lake sediment and produce long stems with leaves floating on the water surface.

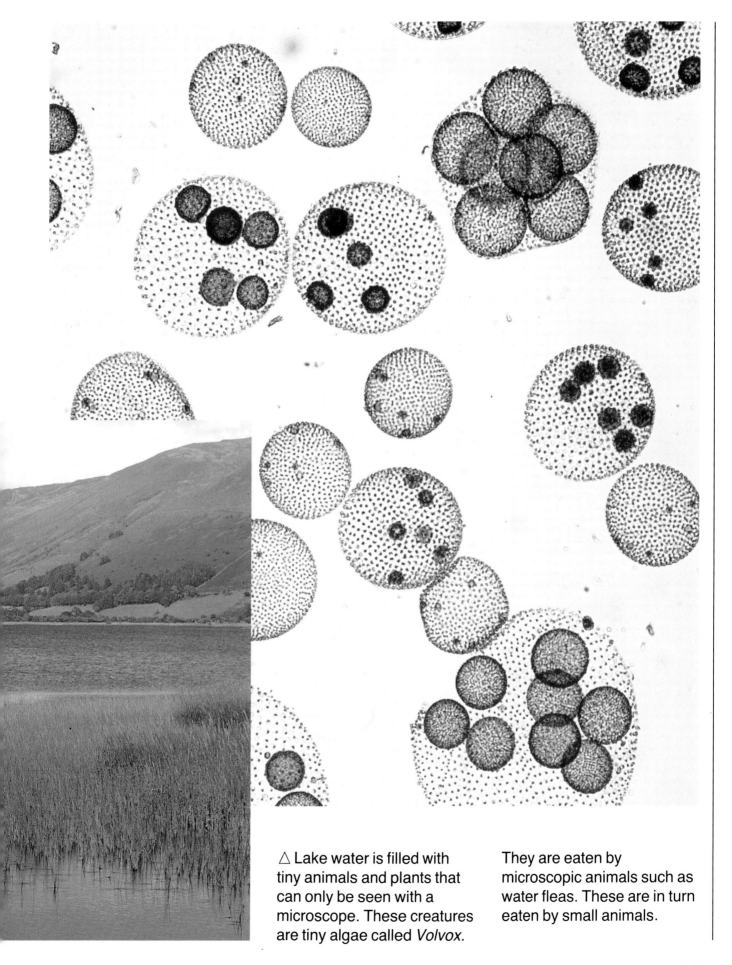

△ Lake water is filled with tiny animals and plants that can only be seen with a microscope. These creatures are tiny algae called *Volvox*.

They are eaten by microscopic animals such as water fleas. These are in turn eaten by small animals.

Lakes and wildlife

Some quite large animals, such as frogs and fish, live in lakes. We are not always sure how they reach the lakes. If a lake has a river flowing from it, most of the animals will take this route into the lake. Birds wading in rivers nearby may pick up fish eggs with their muddy feet. When the birds paddle in the lake, the eggs fall off. The eggs soon hatch and the lake is filled with fish. Strong winds can sweep up and carry smaller animals from one lake to another.

▽ The many small plants that drift about in lake water often make the water look green. Little fish, for example minnows, swim among the plants and are eaten by birds such as kingfishers and herons, and by larger fish such as pike. Ducks and catfish search for food on the lake floor. Water beetles, dragonfly larvae and frogs feed on the smaller animals.

▷ A wide variety of birds, among them these Black Swans of New Zealand, build their nests and rear their young in lakes. The swans scoop up mouthfuls of lake water, then strain out and eat small leaves, seeds, snails and insects.

Water is constantly flowing in and out of the lake. The glacier has all melted away, but streams and rivers still flow down from the valleys and mountains. These bring down pieces of rock, just as the glacier did.

The lighter rock fragments – sand and silt – are washed into the middle of the lake, where they settle as mud. The heavier pieces – the boulders and gravel – pile up at the river mouths, forming broad deltas along the lake shores.

▷ Sediments washed into a lake by a river can form a delta at the river mouth. Where the water currents are slow, pieces of sand and stone drop on to the delta surface. In this way the delta is built up above the water level of the lake.

▽ A lake supplied with water from rivers becomes smaller and smaller as the deltas around its edge creep inward and fill it up, as here in a lake in the Philippines. Fine sediments form in the center of the lake, and coarse rock material is deposited at the edge.

As the water in the lake becomes quite shallow, the lake dries out from time to time. The depth of the water in the lake depends mainly on the "water table". This is the level of water in the surrounding land. Rocks and soil below the water table are soaked with water. Those above it are quite dry. Lake water readily seeps into these drier rocks. In dry seasons the water table falls below the level of the lake floor. Then the lake dries out.

▷ A good example of a lake that disappears and reappears as the water table falls and rises is this one in the Taurus Mountains, Turkey.

In hot parts of the world, lakes often disappear in the dry season as the Sun heats up the lake water and turns it all into vapor. This process is known as evaporation.

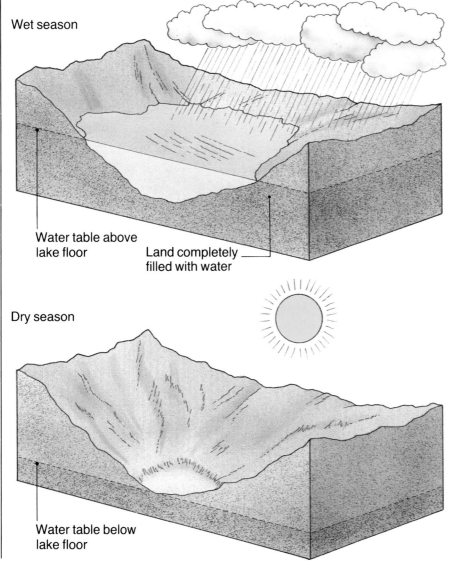

Wet season

Water table above lake floor

Land completely filled with water

Dry season

Water table below lake floor

◁ The land is like a sponge, with tiny holes that can fill with water. The height of the water table marks how far up in the rocks and soil these holes are completely filled.

The lake surface is usually at the same level as the water table. If the water table is above the lake floor, there is water in the lake. In dry spells, the water table – and hence the lake surface – gets lower. If it drops very low, the lake dries out.

At the lowest point around the edge, or rim, of the lake, water flows out as a stream. The running water slowly wears away the rock to form a waterfall and gorge.

As the outlet of the lake is made deeper, more water runs off. The stream becomes wider and soon forms a small river. Loose rocks are carried down by the river. The water splashes and rolls over these to form fast currents called rapids.

◁ At this lake in Switzerland, the amount of water brought down to the lake by streams is too much for the land hollow to hold. A constant flow of water runs off from the lake.

▷ Water draining from a mountain lake often creates waterfalls, gorges and rapids as it flows quickly downhill. As the waterfall cuts back into the bed of the lake, more water drains out and the lake level gets lower. Plants start to grow in the shallows. Gradually the area of open water gets smaller and the patches of plants fill in the lake.

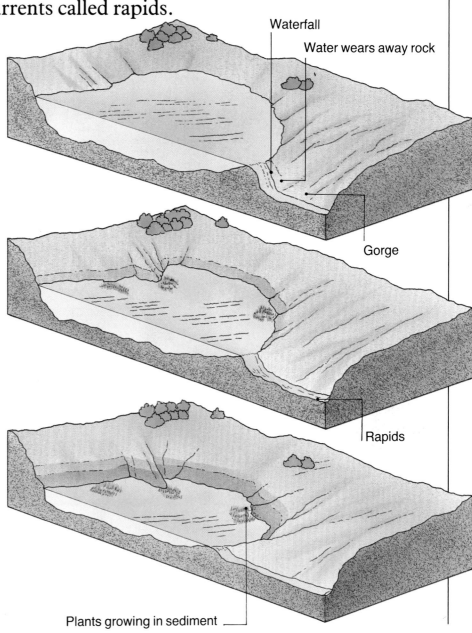

Waterfall

Water wears away rock

Gorge

Rapids

Plants growing in sediment

23

Most of the water has now drained from the lake. The lake floor is filled with mud and gravel. The plants that once grew only around the edge of the lake have spread across almost the whole area.

The leaves, stems and roots of dead plants add to the lake sediment. Some of this plant material does not rot away completely, but builds up thick masses of a spongy brown thread-like, or fibrous, substance called peat.

▷ In this moorland lake, sphagnum moss plants have spread over the surface of the still, shallow waters and formed a soft, wet mat. In this marshy area, grasses and reeds can take root.

Eventually, water-loving trees like willows and alders can take root and grow in the old lake.

▷ The remains of mosses and grasses sink beneath the surface of slowly draining lakes.

Sealed under the water, this plant material does not readily decay because the microscopic creatures that normally rot dead plants – bacteria and fungi – cannot multiply quickly without air. Masses of peat build up.

25

The lake has now dried out completely and the lake floor has all become marshland.

In some places, the mixture of sandy sediment and peat has created a rich, fertile soil. This makes excellent farmland. Tractors, plows and other heavy farm machinery can be driven over the flat ground. Crops can be sown and harvested where there was once water. Only the remains of old beaches prove that the valley was once filled with lake water.

◁ The flat floor of Borrowdale in the Lake District, England, is an ancient lake bed. The land is a good farming area and today is a patchwork of fertile fields.

▽ The huge masses of peat that once lay on the floors of lakes can be a valuable source of fuel. Peat can be burned like coal. In Ireland, for example, some power stations produce electricity from peat.

Blocks of peat can be cut from the land with long spades and carried away by horse and cart. More often, though, huge cutting machines are used to shift hundreds of tons of peat a day.

Lakes and people

Lakes have always been important to people. In areas covered in forest, a lake may be the only open space. Houses are built at the water's edge or in the lake, either on stilts or on artificial islands. People living in lake villages catch and eat the fish that swim in the lake.

Nowadays, many lakes are made artificially by building dams. These lakes are used to store water for drinking or irrigation, or to power generators that produce electricity.

▽ Lake Titicaca, high in the Andes Mountains of Peru, is the second biggest lake in South America. It is 193 km (120 miles) long. Many people live on its shores. They sail its waters in boats made from the reeds that grow along the banks.

△ Reservoirs are artificial
lakes. They are made by
building a wall, or dam,
across a river valley and
letting the valley fill with
water. This reservoir is in
Zimbabwe. The water is used
for irrigation – the watering of
farmland in dry periods – or
for turning machinery.

Glossary

Corrie A hollow on a mountainside where a glacier first forms. The hollow is shaped somewhat like an armchair. When the glacier has completely melted there may be a lake in the bottom of the corrie. A corrie is sometimes called a cirque or a cwm.

Dam A wall formed across a valley that holds back water. A dam may be man-made, or it may be natural, perhaps formed by a landslide.

Delta A triangular area of gravel, mud and silt crossed by water channels, formed at the mouth of a river or melting glacier.

Glacier A river of ice that moves slowly downhill, usually in a valley.

Kame A delta formed at the tip of a glacier and left as a mound when the glacier has all melted away.

Kettle hole A lake formed when a block of ice from a glacier is partly buried in moraine (see below) and then melts.

Marsh An area of permanently wet ground. Any stretches of open water are usually filled with plants such as reeds and moss.

Meltwater Water that forms as ice – particularly glacier ice – melts.

Moraine Rubble, rocks, stones and grit ground away and pulled off the sides of a valley by a glacier. Moraine is carried along by the glacier and eventually dropped on the valley floor as the ice melts.

Peat A brown fibrous substance formed as dead plant material partially decays.

Rapids A region of rough, fast-flowing water where a river flows over rocks and boulders.

Reservoir An artificial lake, constructed to hold water for drinking, irrigation, or generating electricity.

Sediment A mixture of grit, sand and mud forming a thick paste-like layer on the bottom of a lake or river.

Silt Fine particles of soil washed along by a river.

Varves Banded layers of mud and sand formed at the bottom of a lake. Each band represents the rock and soil particles washed into the lake in one summer or winter period.

Water table The level to which the rocks and soil of the land are filled with water. The water table rises following heavy rains and falls during prolonged dry spells. This affects the amount of water in a lake.

Facts about lakes

Largest lake The Caspian Sea in southern USSR is the largest inland body of water in the world. In fact, it is an inland sea, being filled with salt water. It covers an area of 371,000 sq km (143,240 sq miles).

Largest freshwater lake Lake Superior, one of the Great Lakes of North America, has the largest surface area of fresh water. It covers an area of 82,350 sq km (31,800 sq miles).

Deepest lake Lake Bikal, in central Asia, is the deepest lake known. At its center its depth is 1,620 m (5,314 ft).

Highest lake Lake Manasarowar in Western Tibet lies more than 7,620 m (25,000 ft) above sea level.

Underground lake In the Craighead Caverns, Tennessee, USA, some 90 m (300 ft) below ground, is the world's largest underground lake. It has an area of about 1.8 hectares (4½ acres).

Largest reservoir Lake Volta in Ghana, West Africa, is the world's largest artificial lake measured by surface area. It has an area of 8,480 sq km (3,275 sq miles), and the distance round the edge of the lake is 7,250 km (4,500 miles).

Largest dam The Grand Coulee Dam, Washington State, is the world's largest man-made dam. It is 167 m (550 ft) high and 1,270 m (4,170 ft) long along its curved top, or crest.

▷ The importance of lakes to people is well seen at this town, Hallstadt, built by a lake in Austria. Not only is there a town at the water's edge today, but archaeologists have found remains of villages on the same site dating back to the Iron Age, 3,000 years ago. The ancient people must have fished here and paddled across the water in canoes cut from tree logs.

Index

PRINTED IN BELGIUM BY
proost
INTERNATIONAL BOOK PRODUCTION